I CAN COUNT TO 100...
Can You?

A Random House PICTUREBACK®

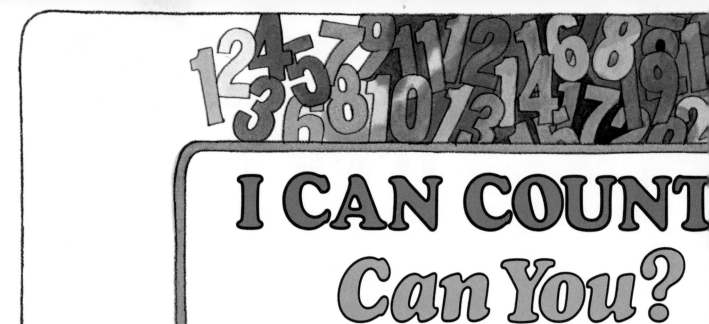

I CAN COUNT
Can You?

by Katherine Howard

with pictures by Michael J. Smollin

RANDOM HOUSE 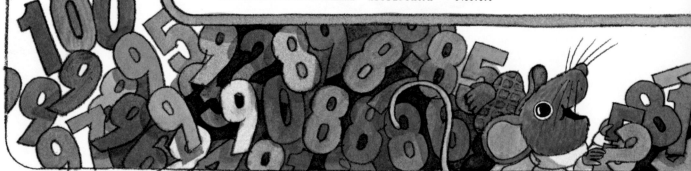 NEW YORK

Copyright © 1979 by Random House, Inc. All rights reserved under International and Pan-American Copyright Conventions. Published in the United States by Random House, Inc., New York, and simultaneously in Canada by Random House of Canada Limited, Toronto.

Library of Congress Cataloging in Publication Data: Howard, Katherine. I can count to 100. SUMMARY: A friendly mouse introduces the numbers from 1 to 100. 1. Counting–Juvenile literature. [1. Counting] I. Smollin, Michael. II. Title. QA113.H68 513′.2 78–62700 ISBN: 0–394–84089–5 (B.C.); 0–394–84090–9 (trade); 0–394–94090–3 (lib. bdg.).

Manufactured in the United States of America. A B C D E F G H I J K 3 4 5 6 7 8 9 0

1
one

I am a mouse and I can count.
I can help you count, too.
It takes practice. But it's not hard.
I can count **one** big ball.
I can count **one** turtle with a sweater on.
Can you count **one** hungry worm?

2
two

Here I am in my sailboat.
I can count **two** frogs.
I can count **two** logs.
Count the frogs. One, **two.**

3
three

I can count **three** railroad cars
standing in front of the station.
I can count **three** mice passengers—
one in each of the railroad cars.
Count the railroad cars. One, two, **three**.
Can you count **three** of something else?

4
four

Here are **four** tugboats.
Two are green and two are red.
Can you count them? One, two, three, **four.**
Can you count **four** tugboat captains?
Don't forget to count the captain who is taking a nap!

5
five

These gloves each have **five** fingers.
Please count the fingers.
One, two, three, four, **five.**
Can you count **five** busy mice?
Don't count me!

6
six

I can count **six** airplanes.
One airplane is upside down.
I can count **six** mice pilots.
Can you count the pilots?
One, two, three, four, five, **six.**
Can you count **six** birds?

7
seven

Here are **seven** giant crayons.
Here are **seven** busy artists
coloring **seven** pictures.
Can you count the giant crayons? Try it.
One, two, three, four, five, six, **seven.**

8
eight

The octopus has **eight** arms.
How many flags does
he have? Count them.
One, two, three,
four, five, six,
seven, **eight.**
Eight flags!
Can you count **eight** fish?

9
nine

Can you count **nine** nice nesting eggs?
Start with the biggest egg. One, two, three, four,
five, six, seven, eight, **nine. Nine** nesting eggs.
There are **nine** mice among the eggs. Count them.
Be careful! Some of the mice are hiding!

10
ten

One toy soldier is lying down.
How many soldiers are
standing up?
Did you count nine?
You're right!
Now count all the soldiers.
One, two, three, four, five,
six, seven, eight, nine, **ten!**
Ten toy soldiers.

6 7 8 9 10

Now that you can count to ten, practice counting over again.

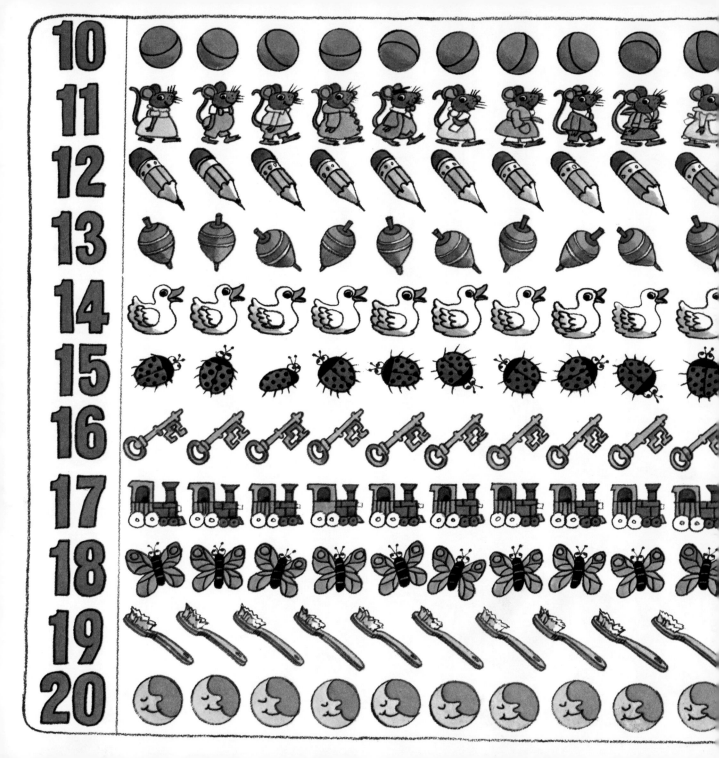

en balls

Eleven mice

Twelve pencils

Thirteen tops

Fourteen ducks

Fifteen ladybugs

Sixteen keys

Seventeen locomotives

Eighteen butterflies

Nineteen
toothbrushes

Twenty
moons

If you want to count to **twenty**,
I'll help you.
Start at the top of the page.

After twenty comes twenty-one. Count the balls and see. After twenty-one comes twenty-two. Now try counting to **thirty**.

20 + 1 = 21

20 + 2 = 22

20 + 3 = 23

20 + 4 = 24

20 + 5 = 25

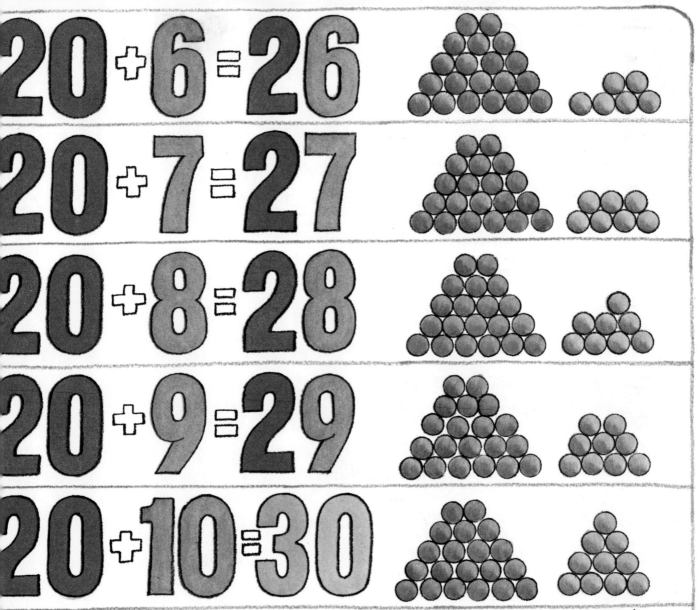

20 + 6 = 26

20 + 7 = 27

20 + 8 = 28

20 + 9 = 29

20 + 10 = 30

You can count to ten. You can count to twenty.
You can count to **thirty.** If you want to count
to one hundred, please turn the page. . . .

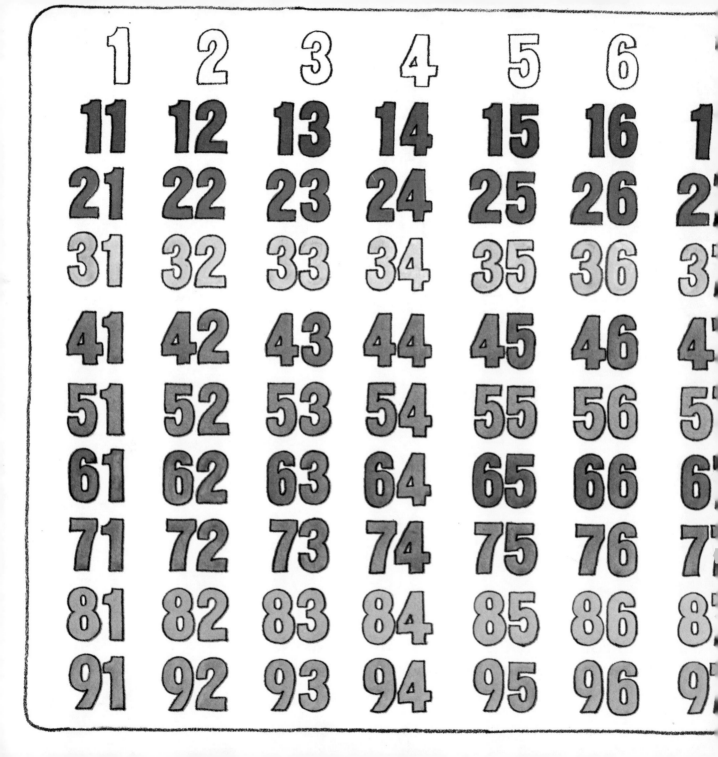

8	9	10...**ten**
18	19	20...**twenty**
28	29	30...**thirty**
38	39	40...**forty**
48	49	50...**fifty**
58	59	60...**sixty**
68	69	70...**seventy**
78	79	80...**eighty**
88	89	90...**ninety**
98	99	100...**one-hundred !**

OH, NO! HERE'S
ONE HUNDRED!
I can count
to **one hundred.**
Can you?
I think you're ready.
Let's try it.
Start with one. . . .

HOORAY!
WE DID IT!
We counted to
one hundred!

Now try
counting to 100
by yourself.